AF598885

RISING FROM THE RUBBLE

THE RESTORATION OF BOLDT CASTLE 1977-2002

Gerald Borland and Hope Irvin Marston
with Dale and Carol Fikes

SECANT PUBLISHING
Salisbury, Maryland

Copyright © 2020 by Hope Irvin Marston
All Rights Reserved

ISBN: 978-1-944962-89-0 (print)
ISBN: 978-1-944962-90-6 (ebook)

www.secantpublishing.com

615 North Pinehurst Avenue
Salisbury MD 21801

Second Printing 2021
First Printing 2020

Cover photo by Patrick Danforth, photographer
www.patrickdanforth.com

Back cover photos by Shelly Gleisner

DEDICATION
(Dale)

Our team effort accomplished much
in the first 25 years.

To my wife Carol and my family, who put up
with my long hours away from them.

To Russel Wilcox, the Thousand Islands Bridge
Authority's Executive Director, and the
TIBA Board Members at the time I was hired.

To Richard Schwerzman, TIBA's legal counsel, who
had a tremendous amount of knowledge in the
building trades and who helped me with organization.

To Jim Bacon, who was such a great help
anywhere he was needed.

To all the bridge employees who worked with me.
Without these people there would be no Dale
Fikes story of Boldt Castle. "Go, Team!"

DEDICATION
(Jerry and Hope)

In Lovely Memory of

Norma P. Borland

and

Arthur W. Marston

Contents

DALE'S LABOR OF LOVE

Because of his deep love for his wife Louise, in 1900 millionaire hotel magnate, George C. Boldt, began building a castle on the St. Lawrence River, located in the heart of the Thousand Islands. He designed his love gift to rival beautiful European castles. Three hundred workers were hired to build the 120-room structure. George planned to give the castle to his beautiful wife as a Valentine's Day gift. The castle would become their summer dream home.

When George purchased his island home, it was called Hart Island. Because of his devotion to Louise, he changed the spelling to Heart Island.

Symbolic of their love for each other, he included hearts most everywhere in the architecture of the castle. To carry out his heart theme, he also had the sea walls on his island re-shaped to make it look like a heart.

The heart in the center of the Boldt Coat of Arms is entwined with two clover sprigs. Perhaps they represented their children entwined as brother and sister.

The clover motif figured prominently in George Boldt's story. Because of George's skillful management of one of the larger hotels on the Hudson River, the hotel's profits grew substantially and so did his prestige. In 1876 he was hired as assistant manager of the renowned Philadelphia Club. A few years later he established the Bellevue Hotel of Philadelphia and his reputation for quality soared.

George was aware of the prestigious Clover Club. Consequently, he invited the members to hold one of their regular meetings at the Bellevue. They were so impressed with the hotel that they scheduled their future dinners there.

George and Louise showed their appreciation for their support by naming their daughter Louise Clover Boldt. But they called her "Clover."

The cloverleaf became part of the Boldt Coat of Arms and several other generations of Boldts chose to name their children Clover.

The Boldts also named their steamboat "Clover."

Dale F. Fikes had the privilege of meeting George Boldt's granddaughter, Louise Clover Boldt Baird, at her summer home on Wellesley Island. She had invited him to tea around 1980 at Hopewell Hall. When he announced his presence at the appointed hour, the elderly lady's nurse escorted him into a large dining room. "You must take your leave of Mrs. Baird in twenty minutes," she admonished.

Not wanting to overstay, Dale kept his eye on the clock. In precisely twenty minutes, he stood to thank his hostess for her time and graciousness. "Please sit down," said Mrs. Baird, "so we can visit some more."

She nodded toward the table and said, "My grandparents purchased this dining room table for the castle." She paused as if composing her thoughts carefully. "When I pass, I want it to go there. Assuming the castle is secure enough at that time."

A few weeks later, Dale and Shane Sanford, who by then was castle manager, were invited to Hopewell Hall again. Upon their arrival they were introduced to Mrs. Baird's daughter Clover, as well as another family member with the same name. Turning to her daughter, Mrs. Baird said, "After I'm gone, I want my dining room table and chairs to go to the castle."

Her daughter nodded in agreement. "That's a lovely idea," she said. "But why not include all of the dining room furniture?" She paused and then added, "And your fine china with the clovers on the border, too?"

"Of course," Mrs. Baird responded, smiling.

Mrs. Baird passed in 1993. Her family honored her wishes and donated the dining room furniture to the Thousand Islands Bridge Authority.

Today's visitors to the restored dining room on the first floor of the castle will appreciate its rich reddish-brown mahogany-like sapele walls and ceiling beams. The fireplace has been restored with a mahogany mantel.

In keeping with the Boldts' hospitality, there's a long table meticulously prepared for twelve guests. Diners will sit comfortably on chairs with tapestry covered seats and slipcovers.

They'll have plenty of elbow room as they break bread together using the Boldt's fine clover patterned china.

The one thing missing from the restored dining room is the button on the floor installed to call the staff if something were needed in the dining room.

****

Unfortunately, in 1904, just a year and a half before the castle would have been completed, Louise Kerher Boldt passed away unexpectedly at age forty-two. She and George had married when she was fifteen and he was twenty-six. At the time of her passing, they had been together for twenty-six years.

Grief-stricken, George contacted the builders of his castle with word of her death. "Stop all construction immediately," he ordered.

His directive was followed, and he never returned to Heart Island. His entire holdings were left vacant and unattended for seventy-three years.

In 1922 Edward J. Noble purchased the entire Boldt Estate. Unfortunately, maintenance and cleanup were minimal until 1977 when Dale Fikes came on the scene.

CHAPTER 1

IN THE BEGINNING…

Dale Frances Fikes, a native of Philadelphia, New York, joined the Carpenters Union Apprenticeship Program in 1962. After four years of learning the trade he worked as a carpenter, a foreman, and then in Construction Management. Thanks to an excellent contractor, he became a journeyman carpenter. He worked with Joe Moran, TIBA's architect, on several construction projects.

Joe appreciated Dale's skills. In 1976 he introduced him to the TIBA's Executive Director and its seven board members. The group unanimously accepted Dale as Clerk of the Works for the new Customs and Immigration Naturalization Services facility they were building on Wellesley Island. In addition to the operations of the new building, Dale would be responsible for custodial services, snow removal, and building maintenance.

While this construction was taking place, the Chambers of Commerce in Alexandria Bay and Clayton expressed their concerns about the deterioration of Boldt Castle. Their greatest fear was that this venerable landmark would be condemned as unsafe and closed to the public.

Those fears were allayed when the E.J. Noble Foundation,

owner of the Boldt Properties, gifted them to the Thousand Islands Bridge Authority (TIBA). Fortunately, by this time the new Customs and Immigration building was ninety percent completed. TIBA was now the owner of Boldt Castle, the Yacht House, the Thousand Islands Club, an 18-hole golf course, the ProShop, several other buildings, and approximately 1,200 acres of land on Wellesley Island.

Dale began working for TIBA on November 1, 1977. His first responsibility was to finish the new Customs and Immigration building and to assist Russel Wilcox, Executive Director, in staffing it. The two quickly developed respect and appreciation for each other.

One spring morning, Russel sent for Dale to come to the Bridge Office to discuss some matter. When he arrived, Joyce Clark, TIBA's secretary, was working on her monthly report on the Customs Building. Sensing she was having a bit of a struggle, he offered to help.

Mrs. Clark appreciated Dale's help. Thereafter, he showed up in her office each month on the day she was finalizing her report. In due time, he wrote them for her, freeing her to tend to her other responsibilities.

Russel soon realized who was writing the monthly reports. Subsequently, he invited Dale to come in and give them orally to the TIBA Board of Directors.

The board members appreciated Dale's philosophy that what needed to be done could be accomplished. When asked to do something he didn't know how to do, he wasted no time in finding out. Subsequently, while working for TIBA, he learned to weld and to work with stained glass.

When the Customs Building was completed, Dale turned his attention to the other Boldt properties. TIBA hired Jim Bacon to help organize the work and acquire the staff needed to work on the Wellesley Island properties, allowing Dale to give his full attention to the castle.

Once they had their chosen crew on board there was no time to waste. "The Thousand Islands Club with its restaurant and rental rooms and the golf course need to be ready for opening to the public by the end of May," Russel told them. Turning to Dale he said, "It's time I take you to the castle to see what must be done immediately."

CHAPTER 2

DALE'S SHOCK

It was mid-December and the ice was not yet strong enough to hold their weight, so TIBA hired an air boat operator to take them about 2,000 feet across the ice from the Yacht House to the castle. Since this was Dale's first visit, he had no idea what to expect. He was about to experience the shock of his life.

When the workers moved out, the pigeons immediately seized the castle and established residence. Thereafter, every building on Heart Island entered a moldering period for more than seventy years. During that time each structure endured tremendous slow deterioration and destruction by Mother Nature, as one-by-one their roofs were blown off or portions collapsed due to the ravages of wind, rain, and snow.

It appeared to Dale that during those years nearly every window had been broken. Nothing had kept the rains out. Each winter the snow had piled up inside, and when it melted in the spring, the water damaged the ceilings, walls, and floors. Now the snow measured a few inches in some rooms and a couple of feet in others.

The ornate ceilings were water-stained; the plastered wall panels had been mutilated; and the wooden floors had rotted.

Consequently, every room was filled with broken glass, chunks of plaster, and rotted wood. But that was just one cause of the disastrous condition of all the Heart Island structures.

In 1918 the castle was opened to the public as a tourist attraction and tour boats began coming daily. Since there had been no maintenance for fourteen years, the entry fees would help pay for the cleanup.

That welcoming gesture triggered some fifty years of continual vandalism, devastation, and theft. The unprotected building was an open invitation to the curious who'd never been inside it.

Weather permitting, anyone who owned a watercraft along the St. Lawrence River could visit the castle. Many folks from the Alexandria Bay area and Canada seized the opportunity to see up close what things looked like. And tour boats began bringing sightseers. Through the years thousands of people from near and far visited the gigantic landmark.

Unfortunately, numbered among them were vandals whose motives could have stemmed from ignorance of the importance of historical sites. Or a gross disregard for their heritage. Some might have been pranksters "showing their guts" to impress their peers. For others, destroying property allowed them to vent their anger or anxieties.

Though frustration and alcohol are precursors to vandalism, that was probably not the situation at the castle. While some beer bottles and cans were found in the rubble when it was cleaned out, there was no appreciable amount.

However, graffiti has been a way of acknowledging one's presence since before the Stone Age. Blank walls are irresistible to those longing to mark their presence. If they happen to be plastered white, as was the situation with the unfinished walls in the castle and in Alster Tower, they are targeted.

Even today in the unpainted sections, one finds fading graffiti that could have been scrawled on the walls fifty years ago. Some of it once stretched from floor to the highest ceiling.

Though graffiti has no merits of its own, it was not surprising to discover in the castle "Kilroy was here!" (A graffiti doodle from World War II.)

Theft was also another problem. Anything of value that was not nailed down was stolen.

However, not everything that disappeared from the castle was taken by thieves. In October 1942, Edward J. Noble, new owner of the Boldt properties, hired Sam Wallins of Watertown to salvage whatever metal he could find to support the war effort. Mr. Wallins' workers stripped the castle of radiators, two large boilers, and thousands of feet of steam pipe. Two large tanks intended for water reservoirs were also removed as well as all the decorative iron work, and the elaborate heating system.

Harold Comstock, Superintendent of the Thousand Islands Estate, estimated that thirty to forty tons of iron and steel were salvaged in that process.

Russel and Dale left the castle to check out the other structures on Heart Island. When their sobering tour ended, he turned to Dale and asked, "What do you think?"

Dale looked him in the eyes, paused, and said, "I could not have screwed things up more than they already are!"

Twenty-five years of hectic days and sleepless nights began as Dale assumed responsibility for restoration of the castle.

What follows is the story of this talented man whose work ethic and dedication to the castle were incomparable as demonstrated in how he engineered the cleanup, rebuilding, and restoration during the first decades of returning it to its intended glory.

CHAPTER 3

BOLDT CASTLE DETERIORATION

The restoration of Boldt Castle presented several challenges. The extent of the destruction was the first one. The second was the weather limitations. During early winter and late spring, ice conditions made it impossible to reach the castle. TIBA's goal was to open the grounds to the public by mid-May. Top priority of the management was to make the castle safe for the thousands of guests expected to visit before the season ended.

When the restoration began in 1978, the first chore was to remove about two feet of snow inside the castle walls. Then the rubble left by the ravages of the weather and vandals must be cleared away. Glass shards had accumulated inside and outside from the castle's 348 broken windows as the rain and snow poured in year after year.

Since that devastation had been going on for over seventy years, droppings from hundreds of pigeons added a considerable amount of debris that needed to be shoveled up.

In many rooms, dunes of powdered plaster had grown higher and higher through the years and broken glass blanketed the rotted wooden floors. In addition to wearing heavy work gloves and warm boots, the men always put on dust masks before tackling the mess that needed to be cleared out.

The wood and anything else that was burnable was chopped up. After assuring the safety of the fireplaces, the crew burned it. Not only did that get it out of their way, the warm glow from the fire created a cheery atmosphere and helped to warm the bitterly cold interior of the castle.

Anything salvageable was saved in crates, and that included sixty-one doors! Some things were kept as patterns for replacement.

In addition to this clutter that needed to be picked up and disposed of, three floors of the elevator shaft were filled with dozens of empty five-gallon tar pails left behind when the flat roofs had been patched.

Once the men began work, the air was thick with a trillion dust particles that could not be contained.

The restoration crew set to work shoveling smaller items like broken glass and plaster into the tar pails and lugging them downstairs. Larger items were tossed out the windows and loaded into a utility trailer. The trailer hauled them down to the Swan Pond with the lawn tractor. They would be carried away by barge later.

The massive cleanup operation began in January 1978 with the small staff that had been hired for the job. Assisted by men and women from the CETA (Comprehensive Employment Training Act) program, work began on the castle and Alster

Tower. Fallen plaster and broken glass layered the rotted floors, making it difficult to find a place to put their feet. Every bit had to be picked up and thrown out the window or carried outside.

While some men were tackling the castle rubble, others worked through a similar challenge in other buildings.

The castle had to be open to the public to celebrate the Canadian and American holidays. How could all this devastation be cleaned up by the end of May?

CHAPTER 4

THE BOLDT YACHT HOUSE

Built in 1899, the Yacht House became the center of Boldt's activities in the area. Canals connected to the Boldt farms allowed produce to be packed in ice and transported by barge to Clayton. Daily trains transported it to Boldt's hotels in New York City and Philadelphia. The family's watercraft were housed here, as were the captain and crew.

A boat-building shop was also established to build first-class speed boats and pleasure craft. A vent with a tall cap could be lowered over a steamboat funnel, preventing damage from sparks and boiler fire smoke.

As with all Boldts' holdings on the river, the Yacht House fell into disrepair. The roofs leaked, the windows were broken, and there was general deterioration inside and out. Water had rotted anything made of wood. The docks had also deteriorated.

The Yacht House, located about 2,000 feet across open water from Boldt Castle on Hart Island, became the home base for the castle restoration work.

In January 1978 Dale hired a small crew and set up space there as a base of operations, complete with a heated lunch room and coffee pot. The crew gathered here each morning to plan the day's work. It was also a place to come in and get warm after spending time at the castle. The men walked over to the castle on ice using a lawn tractor and a utility trailer to carry their tools. The chains on the tractor tires gave traction on the ice.

During weak ice conditions the men worked at repairing the docks, making them ready for daily use. The foundation and the docks were built on the traditional stone-filled timber cribs of the era. The cribs that remained submerged were still sound.

However, the top two or three feet of timbers had rotted from exposure to the air as the water levels varied. They had to be removed and replaced on the forty cribs. Visitors can see those cribs when visiting the Yacht House. In addition, the rotted framing and decking were removed and replaced.

All materials for the work at the castle had been delivered to the Yacht House. Later they were transported there.

Meanwhile, contractors with special equipment worked with the crew to complete the elevated work at the Yacht House, and plumbers were hired to install bathroom fixtures, etc.

Work on restoring the Yacht House began in 1978 and continued seasonally thereafter until 1996, when it was opened to the public. The living quarters on the upper floor were originally occupied by the captain and his crew. Later they were home to the Noble Foundation caretaker. Now they were opened for viewing. Visitors to Boldt Castle could reach the Yacht House by a regularly scheduled shuttle boat between the two locations.

As work progressed on the castle, the windows were being made at the Yacht House. Elliott "Manny" Slate was the foreman for this work with Dale Leeson as lead carpenter.

Today's visitors to the Yacht House will see an historic 48-star flag suspended over the boat slips. This flag was a gift from Andy Rae, World War II veteran.

The Yacht House continues to be central in the Boldt Castle restoration because it is the main link to the castle. Workboats, tools, and materials are stored here.

THE WINDOWS

Window frames without glass are soon destroyed by the elements. The original white oak window frames were still good; only the sashes had to be replaced.

Machines needed to build the replacements were set up in the Yacht House workshop. Manny Slate was in charge as the work began.

Since the windows varied in sizes and shapes, patterns and special jigs were needed. Working together, Manny Slate, Dale Leeson, and Brian Salisbury were soon producing fine quality cedar windows.

With an estimated 348 windows in the castle alone, this would be a very time-consuming undertaking. They needed more help.

An assembly line of jigs was set up to make the window sashes. Arched windows were made by laminating strips together to create the proper shapes. Richard Dack and Ken Hunter joined the shop crew to lend a hand. They used Plexiglas instead of glass for the sake of endurance.

The completed window sash was then given two coats of stain. It was now ready to be installed in the castle.

CHAPTER 5

THE CLEAN-UP BEGINS

Though it seemed impossible to get everything done and taken care of, at no time did Dale consider not opening the castle on schedule. The tourism industry needed that to happen and he'd move heaven and earth to see that it did.

These weighty matters kept Dale awake at night. The castle had to be open to the public to celebrate the Canadian and American holidays. How could all this work be accomplished so quickly?

He faced two monumental challenges. One was to make the castle presentable for the public. The other was to be sure the buildings and grounds were safe for the thousands of guests from around the world who visited each year.

Falling roof tiles had to be picked up. Downed trees littering the ground must be disposed of. The docks wanted for repair. And the concession stand must be cleaned and painted.

Dale and his crew set to work to accomplish what seemed like miracles. They had worked three months cleaning out the castle. Much more needed to be done inside, but at least it was a safe place to visit. Further restoration would have to wait until the castle closed to the public in late October.

Opening day was about six weeks away. Other areas of Heart Island needed to be cleaned up to ensure the safety of the visitors who would be pouring off the tour boats to visit Boldt Castle near the end of May.

Due to Dale's planning and the hard work of everyone involved, enough had been done to allow the castle to open safely for Victoria Day and Memorial Day.

Word spread that the Thousand Islands Bridge Authority had taken over Boldt Castle and its properties and was working to restore them. Visitors were welcome to come see what had been accomplished.

The new season opened on May 22, 1977, and an overwhelming number of tourists showed up that first year. These visitors appreciated the changes that had been made since their previous visits. By closing day in mid-October, about 90,000 visitors from around the world had been shuttled across the St. Lawrence River to visit Boldt Castle. The concession stand scarcely had room to operate and long lines stretched across the dock from the two small restrooms.

That fall, a larger facility was built on the dock. The concession building was renovated into a fast-food type service to accommodate the guests' brief time for eating due to the tour boat schedules.

Visitors to Heart Island enjoyed making friends with the scampering squirrels that abounded everywhere. But the delightful wild animals became pests as tourists encouraged them with popcorn treats. When popcorn fell into the water accidentally, or was tossed in, it attracted the carp also.

As with the squirrels, the carp were soon tamed. The sound of tour boats signaled it was chow time and they followed the boats to the dock.

Their stocky bodies ranged from one to three feet and they were covered with scales the size of silver dollars. Because they were bottom feeders and their color blended with the cloudy water, it was hard to see them until their eagerness to get a free meal brought them to the surface in search of popcorn. Of course, this delighted the onlookers, especially the children.

Perhaps local anglers should use popcorn for bait.

From the time the castle first welcomed the tour boats, the cashiers operated in enclosures that looked like giant bird cages. Consequently, working at the mercy of the elements was occasionally unpleasant. The larger, new building provided indoor facilities for them, along with speedier service.

Two of the boat companies were now using larger boats to carry guests to the castle. These expanded facilities were put to good use when the next year's attendance grew to 110,000 patrons. But more docks would have to be constructed to accommodate the larger numbers.

However, it would take many years to restore the Grand Hall and Stairway in the castle because the work could not be done during the busy tourist season.

CHAPTER 6

THE DIAMOND

One afternoon a group of visitors waiting to board their tour boat was startled by a sudden shriek. As Dale hurried to the dock to see what was going on, a lady was shaking one hand and sobbing uncontrollably. In the other, she clutched a melting chocolate ice cream cone as she peered down at the floorboards.

"What's the problem, ma'am?" Dale asked.

"I've lost my diamond ring," she wailed.

"Where did you lose it?"

"Right there!" She pointed toward the deck. "It went through that crack in the boards!"

"We'll find it for you," Dale answered. He bent down and shined his flashlight through the crack while the distraught woman continued to sob. When he saw the ring, he beckoned to one of the dockhands.

"Go down under the dock and I'll hold my light to mark the spot."

Feeling reassured that she'd get her ring back, the sobbing lady told him the ring was too loose.

"That's why it slipped off my finger." She wiped her eyes and added, "That ring is very special to me. I intended to get it resized when I got back home."

The dock boy returned shortly with the ring, returned it to its owner, and went back to his work. When the lady turned to thank him, he was gone. Turning to Dale she said, "I'm grateful to get my ring back. I want to give you a generous tip."

"Thank you, ma'am, but that isn't necessary," Dale replied.

"However, if you wish to leave something for the dock boy, I'm sure he'd be pleased because he has a huge college debt."

CHAPTER 7

HELP WITH THE CLEAN-UP

While his men were working to empty the castle of the mess they'd found throughout, Dale compiled a list of materials required to spruce things up and begin the restoration process. He wanted to have what they needed on hand when the ice left the river. After running these matters through his mind, he considered how they'd get these supplies over to the castle. Unfortunately, there was no way to back a delivery truck up to the island. Hmmm?

He solved that problem by purchasing a homemade pontoon boat to get the materials to their destination. This hybrid vehicle was made of 18-inch culvert pipe filled with foam for flotation purposes. It had nose cones on one end and a bracket at the back to carry a 25 HP outboard motor. The treated plywood floor deck was adequate for his needs, and eventually it carried many a load across the water to Heart Island.

Previously, ramps had been built from the ground up to their homemade pontoon boat. The pontoon carried its load over to the boat slip behind the Yacht Boat House and emptied it there until there was enough to fill the dump truck.

After emptying the castle of what needed to be thrown out,

the workmen repaired the flooring enough to make the rooms safe. They created handrails where needed, cordoned off areas that were unsafe, and tidied up as best they could in the time they had.

Once the required materials were brought to the island, they needed to be hauled up the hill, several hundred feet, to the castle. Light supplies could be carried by hand while others would be loaded into a wheelbarrow. With very heavy loads, one person pushed from behind while another man in front pulled with a rope. Not exactly high tech!

The men gathered up downed trees, limbs, leaves, and general debris. Some of them cut brush while others tackled the tall grass. Planning for the days ahead, they purchased a tractor with a mower to have on hand as soon as it was needed. Because time was growing short before the castle was scheduled to be opened to the public, they closed off or barricaded some areas for safety from falling roof tiles.

Dale's friend Jim Bacon, the man in charge of TIBA's equipment, buildings and grounds on the U.S. mainland, built them a heavy-duty utility trailer for use with the tractor. Cheers rang out when the crew heard the news. No longer would they endure that backbreaking work of hauling their materials up the hill to the castle. And no more lugging the debris down to the barge that would carry it back to the mainland.

CHAPTER 8

MIN AND THE WAR HORSE

TIBA furnished a steel-hulled inboard boat for the crew to get to work at the castle. One morning Dale couldn't get the engine running. His patience was giving out rather loudly when Min Hartman passed by. At that time, Min oversaw the cashiers. She had grown up on the river, and she knew how to handle people and boats. Seeing Dale's frustration, she said, "Let me give it a try."

Min soon had that old War Horse purring like a kitten. "Don't forget to choke it," she added as she hurried off to her office.

"I'll remember," Dale promised. Meanwhile, that leaky old boat was soon replaced by some aluminum outboard boats.

Min was not the only woman who contributed to the restoration work. Several others, including retired women, worked hand in hand with the contractors as plasterers, electricians, or laborers where needed. One of the plasterers was a woman whose work was commendable and there was an excellent female electrician on the job. Retired women volunteers also lent their hands.

CHAPTER 9

REBUILDING THE DOCKS

The 90,000 visitors to the castle the first year it opened to the public arrived there by boat from Alexandria Bay and Clayton, New York, and from Rockport and Gananoque, Canada. Because of the huge crowds, the tour companies had switched to even larger boats to transport them. Consequently, more docks were needed. Plans were made to add about 120 feet of dockage, angled toward the Power House, making it easier for the boats to land.

The U.S. Army Corps of Engineers approved the plans to support the dock on cribs built of heavy timbers filled with tons of stones. This was a major undertaking. The field office in the old customs building became a hub of activity for the dock job. With temperatures hovering at zero or below, it was essential to have a warm area nearby and to ensure a change of dry clothing was handy. Gloves always needed to be dried, so extra ones were kept on hand as well as outer garments of various types. In addition, coffee breaks and lunches were available in the heated shelter.

Before beginning to build cribs on the ice, the location and bottom contour of the river bottom had to be determined.

First, the size of each one was marked on the ice and a hole was bored on all four corners. The depth of water at each one was measured using a long bamboo cane to give an accurate picture of the area where the crib would rest on the riverbed.

All exterior wood was of pressure-treated material. Cribs with solid timber bottoms were constructed according to their individual measurements. In truth, they looked like giant potato crates.

Next came the cold, wet job of cutting the ice around each crib with a chainsaw. The "lucky" man chosen for the task headed off to the field office to don proper gear. When dressed in his water-resistant suit over his heavy insulated work clothes, he resembled an astronaut spacewalker.

Flying ice chips mixed with water freeze hard overnight. The result was an extremely rough, slippery work area. A footprint left in slush became a stumbling block by morning. When the workers returned to the job, they must remember that.

The men wore gloves to protect their hands from the cold, and to keep their fingers from being pinched. These were necessary precautions as they carried stones the size of bowling balls or basketballs, weighing as much as 100 pounds, from the truck to the crate.

Despite the cold, the brawny rock handlers worked up a sweat when they filled the cribs. As the cribs began to sink, more timbers and stones were added. The crew filled the cribs until they rested on the bottom and stood about three feet above the level of the ice. This was necessary because the water levels varied from year to year.

A contractor with an old dump truck hauled the heavy stones over the ice to the cribs from Wellesley Island. If there happened to be soft ice underneath, a dump truck loaded with stones would sink instantly. For safety's sake, the driver's side door was removed to allow quick exit in an emergency.

After the last crib was built, all of them were tied together with large timbers. They would settle in place until the ice went out…usually in late April. Then the crew would return and construct the framing and install the decking.

CHAPTER 10

THE TRACTOR CAPER

Thick ice on the river made it the ideal time for building the new docks as well as doing other winter work. Dale hired Davis Tree Service from Carthage to cut some dangerous dead trees around the island. He borrowed a John Deere tractor from the Parks Department to skid the logs across the ice to Wellesley Island. Jim Bacon's job was to drive this two-cylinder "Popping John," as everyone called it, because it could be heard for miles in the frigid air.

A large iron blade was mounted on the front end of "Popping John" to push away the snow and form an ice road. Dale watched momentarily from his work on the dock as Jim bang-banged his way over the ice.

As he turned back to the work at hand, the sound of the tractor suddenly stopped. The deadly silence was eerie, and foreboding. He glanced up but couldn't see the driver. "Jim's down!" he shouted.

He and his crew dropped everything and charged over the ice running and stumbling to find him. As they approached the scene, they saw the large snow blade had hooked itself on the ice, preventing the tractor from disappearing under the ice.

But where was Jim?

"God, I hope he's okay," Dale muttered.

When they reached him, he was struggling to the surface. "We'll get you out of there," one of them shouted. Grabbing his coat collar, the crew managed to pull him free. One man ran to the Yacht House, called the ambulance, and returned with the station wagon. Jim was quickly loaded in.

Time was of the essence to get him warmed up.

Fearing hypothermia, or possibly shock, the men yanked off their outer clothing and wrapped him like a mummy to keep him from freezing.

As they tore out to meet the ambulance, Jim said in a quivering voice, "My leg was wedged by the brake pedal." He took in a deep breath. "I wrenched my foot trying to get it out of my boot before I froze to death."

When they saw the ambulance coming as they headed down Wellesley Island, the driver pulled the station wagon crossways to block it.

The ambulance screeched to a halt. The driver was ready for a fight. "GET THE HELL OUT OF THE WAY! WE'RE ON A CALL!"

Dale jumped out and responded, "We ARE your call!"

Jim was transferred to the ambulance and taken to the hospital in Alexandria Bay. One of the men called Jim's wife, and the crew began to relax.

“That was the most frightening day of my life,” Dale muttered as the color returned to his weathered face.

Now that Jim was safe, they had to free the borrowed tractor from the ice and return it to the Parks Department before the Department of Environmental Conservation began to complain about it being in the water.

They called a wrecker, and an attempt was made to winch the tractor up a log ramp. That action bent the frame on the wrecker, but it didn’t free the tractor.

Knowing the ice would go out of the river in about three weeks, Dale asked permission to leave it in the water until then. The crew attached a long cable to the tractor, anchoring it to the shore to wait until they could recover it.

In mid-April, the water cleared and the wrecker with its reinforced frame easily towed the tractor out of its watery prison.

TIBA had the tractor reconditioned before returning it to its owners. A short time later, Dale received a call from the Parks Department. The caller had one question.

“Would you be willing to dunk another one of our tractors and refurbish it for us at your shop?”

As for Jim Bacon, he’d had all the log skidding he ever wanted. The rest of the logs were transported by water.

CHAPTER 11

CASTLE RESTORATION BEGINS

Restoration inside the castle began with the Reception Room. Perhaps it was chosen because it was near the main entrance. Or possibly because it was one of the few rooms where the ceiling did not leak. Maybe it was spared that destruction because it was under one of the towers not ravaged by wicked winter weather through the years.

The windows and doors had been boarded up at one time. Eventually vandals broke down the doors. But the room did not suffer from the violent winds and torrential rain that wrecked much of the castle. However, its accessibility, as with all the Boldt properties, had subjected it to theft.

When they found nothing to steal, the vandals turned to destructive behavior, damaging or defacing whatever was within reach. Using their pocket knives, or some other sharp objects, they randomly carved out some of the sphinx-like heads and fleurs-de-lis on the ornate plaster wall panels.

Workmen spent many days repairing the damage, but they didn't know what to do about the wall panels. Earl Rumsey Durand, a visiting artist/sculptor, spent a week at the castle in 1978. When Dale gave him a tour, two things caught his attention. One was the damaged wall panels where the pieces had been indiscriminately gouged out.

Earl's artistic expertise included working with plaster; he knew how to restore those walls. Speaking with Dale the next day, he said, "Bring your crew into the Reception Room and I'll show you how to make a mother mold from the undamaged panels."

Dale wasted no time in gathering the men to see what they could learn. Not wanting to miss a single detail, they gave Earl their rapt attention.

First, he pulled out a fine brush and cleaned the dust from the undamaged section he wanted to copy. When he was certain he'd removed every speck, he sprayed it with a releasing agent. "This will allow us to pull the mold off when it's dry," he said.

Earl waited for that to happen before spraying it with a fast-drying liquid rubber compound. As it dried, he sprayed it again and again until it was covered with a coating about 1/8" thick. Finally, he reinforced his work with Plaster of Paris.

"Thanks to the releasing agent, once that dries, you can peel it off. Then you'll have your mother mold to cast the pieces you need to replace the damaged ones," he added.

After Earl returned home, Dale and his crew wasted no time in casting the pieces they needed. When the last one was finished, Manny Slate, who was one of the foremen working with Dale, set them in place and plastered the area around each one.

Next, they turned their efforts to the floor. Initially throughout the castle all the rotted floors were replaced. But because of the tramp of thousands of feet each season, most every year thereafter every floor had to be repainted and resealed once more.

Finally, the hearth was restored with the addition of a new granite mantel, built by Earl Durand, and new drapes were added for the finishing touch to the room.

The Reception Room opened into the Billiards Room, which could also be entered from the Grand Hall where Durand built a second granite fireplace mantel.

CHAPTER 12

THE BILLIARDS ROOM

After making the Reception Room presentable, safe, and comfortable, Dale and his crew moved on to the adjacent Billiards Room. As with other rooms in the castle, the ceilings were damaged from the annual freeze and thaw conditions. Where they suffered only staining, they were covered over with paint.

However, in the Billiards Room the leaky roof had destroyed about two-thirds of the molded ceiling as well as the plaster wall panels. Their immediate goal was to have things presentable for opening the castle in late May, but there was not enough time for them to do all the required work. Consequently, Dale contracted with GEF Construction to restore the room.

The contractors made molds from the unspoiled panels and sent them to another company to be fabricated.

While awaiting their return, their own men tore up the flooring that had rotted from years of rain and snow blowing in from the broken windows.

After studying the wooden floor designs in exclusive homes at the turn of the previous century as well as other patterns that seemed appropriate for Boldt Castle, they concluded a heavier than usual parquet flooring was most appropriate for the Billiards Room as well as the Dining Room.

The heavy billiard table that had been donated to the castle by the Wilcox family could not be used until it was restored. Dale was personally involved in overseeing its restoration. The Brunswick Company was contacted for help with the project. After hearing the history of the castle and the table, the company's experts responded with tips for restoring it and then generously donated new pockets and felt to cover the slate top.

CHAPTER 13

THE HART

The second thing that had captured Earl Durand's attention was a hart (a European red stag at least five years old) towering atop the roof of the front of the castle. Unfortunately, the deer was missing most of its head and antlers.

Earl couldn't get that decapitated deer out of his mind. He mulled over how the missing parts could be reconstructed. Once he had a plan in mind, he shared it with Dale. "If you can get me the neck section with the cheeks intact, I'll cast a new head for the deer," he promised.

That was too good an offer and too grand a gift to ignore. The restoration crew set to work immediately building a scaffold from the fourth-floor balcony up to the beheaded hart, which stood almost six stories above the ground. They extended a platform over to the deer and cut the neck off at an original joint, brought it down, and gave it to Earl.

Not long afterwards Earl returned home with the neck piece and set to work making a clay mold. After it dried, he cast a new head in bronze, complete with antlers. He returned to the castle the following spring, bringing the bronze hart head with him.

Now came the challenge of getting the 75-pound creation back onto the stag's neck.

First, a hole was drilled in the stag's body and another in the cast head, making certain they were spaced precisely where needed to fit one into the other. A steel pin was epoxied into the head to keep it in place.

Two of Dale's crew carried it up to the fourth-floor balcony and put it into a sling. Then using a rope and pulley system, they raised it to the top of the scaffolding. Working carefully, they pulled it along to the end of the platform they had built previously.

Meanwhile, another crew member climbed the scaffold and mounted the deer, like a bareback rider. With his legs clamped tightly around the stag's body, he epoxied in and around the hole in its neck. Two men lifted the bronze head up to him and he fitted it into place.

Once again, the magnificent hart stood proudly atop the castle. Mission accomplished!

The stained glass colors in the dome represent the blue river border reflecting the sky above and includes the heart of the Boldt family crest. Dale considers this work his “Swan Song”.

The heart motif is prominent throughout the castle and grounds including the iron railing and other iron work.

Photo credit Diane Peebles

The red deer stag, known as a hart, appears in the
Boldt Coat of Arms from the German Heritage.

The Pedestal Light at Alster Tower saved by an anonymous admirer of the castle.

CHAPTER 14

THE CASTLE RESTROOMS

With the rapid increase in attendance, public restrooms became paramount. The decision was made to install them in the same location as was shown in the original castle plans.

To accommodate the increased demand, new potable (drinking) water had to be supplied. This water came from the St. Lawrence River and was filtered and chlorinated to meet New York State's quality standards.

A new wastewater treatment plant also had to be built because of the additional flow. Now, more electrical power was required to meet the added demand.

This expanded water treatment process required a licensed operator. Kevin Gillette, a member of Dale's original crew, stepped up to the plate and took the necessary training. It took about three years to complete this work.

For the safety of the public, the water must be tested every day to ensure it meets the state's water quality standards.

In addition to the quality work Kevin did with the water treatment, he also became licensed by the Coast Guard to operate the Yacht House/Boldt Castle Shuttle. Until about ten years ago, he filled in when the regular captains were not available.

CHAPTER 15

THE GARDENS AND GROUNDS

Admission fees from the increasing number of visitors to Heart Island each year made it possible to increase the budget. When workmen began cleaning the castle and grounds, not much had been done with the upper grounds and the Italian Gardens. Due to the terrain, there was no access to them with the lawn tractor and trailer.

A Bobcat loader was purchased at this time. Though it was the smallest model, the crew now had power, and it was a vast improvement over hauling debris away by wheelbarrow.

The architect suggested removing a portion of the retaining wall to give access to the upper grounds. That is where hundreds of pounds of broken glass and plaster had been dumped when the castle clean-up began because there was no means to carry it elsewhere.

The loader was used to build a ramp from the dock area to the upper grounds. Once it was finished, the machine made many trips to the barge carrying bucket loads of broken glass, plaster, about a hundred tar pails, and other debris that had accumulated once restoration began inside the castle.

The gardens took on a new life when they were free from the mounds of debris. The tall grass was cut with weed-eaters, flowerbeds were established, and clover grew profusely. Quite likely it was first planted there in honor of the Boldts' daughter, Clover.

With these improvements came the need for more help to mow, plant, water, and care for the flowers. Since taking care of the grounds is a seasonal position, college students were hired, as well as senior citizens. Many of these seniors were military veterans, some dating back to World War II. As the gardens were expanded, the demand for more workers grew.

Today, to keep the grounds and gardens beautiful throughout the tourist season, approximately 20,000 plants and flowers are grown annually in the TIBA Greenhouses. About 12,000 more are grown by additional suppliers.

The white marble statuary on the grounds has been added since Dale's retirement in 2002.

CHAPTER 16

MONEY LAUNDERING

The Shell Fountain, located on the lower walkway, is a water-spouting gargoyle backed up by a large marble clamshell. The bowl, which resembled a giant bathtub, was totally in ruins. The workmen rebuilt it and then modernized it with an electrical pump to recirculate the water.

Many tourists considered the fountain to be a wishing well, and few people can resist one of those. From the youngest visitors to the eldest, they tossed in their coins, hoping their wishes would be granted.

Once or twice a season, the fountain was cleaned out. Along with the algae that had formed around the edges, there was a large volume of coins that had been tossed in by visitors. These coins were scooped up with a shovel into five-gallon buckets.

Tourists also considered the swimming pool in the ground level of the castle to be a wishing well. They, too, made their wishes as they tossed their coins into it. This pool was also cleaned out on a yearly schedule and the money picked up.

After giving the coins a hasty rinse with the hose, several muscular summer workers carried the heavy buckets to the ticket booth and left them with the cashier.

A few days later Dale went to see how much money they had collected. When the head cashier saw him coming, she scowled. "What in the world did you expect me to do with those stinking coins?"

"I wanted you to count them!"

"A counting machine must have clean money! I can't put those filthy, wet coins through mine. They were so nasty, I didn't even want to touch them." She snatched a breath and added, "Besides they stunk to high heaven."

She looked him in the eye and delivered her final salvo. Dale knew she was more upset than serious, when she concluded, "If you bring me more cruddy coins, I'm going to shoot you on sight!"

"OH!" said Dale, chagrined. "I'm so sorry. I'll send a couple of fellows over to pick them up."

Several days later the buckets of dirty money were carried back down to the lower area.

Dale and his crew wondered how they'd clean up the stinking money. They decided to scrub it with the strongest detergent they could find. Then they would hose it down.

As soon as he could free up some student help, Dale's crew set up two large screens where the coins could be spread out. The students scoured them with a soapy brush and then hosed them off until the water ran clean. The money looked clean, but it still stunk!

On rainy days, or times when there was less demanding activity, the senior volunteers rolled the offensive coins. Not one of the young workers volunteered to help them.

Eventually the last coin was wrapped, and several men carried the money to the bank. The cashier held her breath as she received the wrapped coins. She counted them as quickly as possible and credited them with the proper amount of cash. "Thank you for the coins," she said. "Now that we've paid you for them, we'll send them to be incinerated."

The reader should take note that this is the only legal way to launder your money.

CHAPTER 17

THE GAZEBO

The Gazebo lay in ruins. Only a few stone steps indicated it had ever existed, and there was no indication of what the roof looked like. The architects created plans to restore it by studying old photographs, while the crew set to work picking up the fragments to be used in recreating the structure.

In due time they rebuilt the crumbled native stone columns using the fragments they had found. The photos were fundamental in determining the shape and details for the roof.

Once the Gazebo was completed, it became a focal point for wedding ceremonies and photos. The proximity to Alster Tower with its grand stairway made it more inviting.

At least seventy weddings are now solemnized on Heart Island each year. Many of the brides choose to make the Gazebo their wedding chapel. Others exchange their vows at the Italian Gardens, in front of the castle, or at the Power House.

However, during the ceremonies the buildings and grounds remain open to the public.

CHAPTER 18

THE GRAND HALL AND THE MARBLE STAIRWAY

As much as possible, restoration work continued during the months when visitors flocked to Heart Island. But by the late 1970s, the tourist traffic was so heavy it had to be curtailed in certain areas open to the public.

The castle was the main attraction, and postponement delayed the restoration. It would take two to three years before the workmen could carry out their initial plans in the most popular places for visitors. The best they could do those first years was to clean things up and repair the floors. The castle was a safe place to visit, though the restoration was scarcely begun.

The Grand Hall and Stairway were in a dreadful condition. The rough stairs and the rickety hand railings were unsafe. The floor was littered with ceiling plaster and underneath, the boards were broken and rotted. Tourists had scrawled graffiti on the walls and woodwork. Unsafe areas were cordoned off.

The focal point in the Grand Hall was now the restored staircase and the white columns on both sides.

The columns were made in two sections and glued together with adhesive. They were mounted on wooden foundations built like some they found in the servants' quarters.

Workmen made molds from the existing panels in the ornate plaster ceiling panels to replace the missing ones.

Meanwhile, architects designed new wood railings and sent their plans to outside millworks to be built.

When the finished work was received, Brian Umstead, local contractor, installed the main stairway railings as well as the new quarter sawn white oak woodwork. Peter Curtis, of Curtis Furniture Company, also did some of the fine millwork. GEF Construction completed additional railings, as well as the ceiling work, over the course of two seasons.

MARBLE STEPS

The stairway had been used by thousands of visitors to the castle since it first opened its doors to the public. When the crew began the work of restoring it, their first job was to remove the old steps and railing from the original steel skeleton.

Gordon Fayhe, a local craftsman with GEF Construction, took measurements and made patterns for all the treads and risers, with special attention given to the curved portions of the steps. The items were purchased from a Vermont marble supplier. Each piece of marble for the stairs was blueprinted and numbered according to its location in the finished stairway.

When the carefully packed pieces arrived at the Yacht House, they were unloaded onto the pontoon barge. At Heart Island they were hauled up to the castle by tractor. Mike Gibbs, a local craftsman, along with GEF Construction, installed the numbered pieces. The work was completed in 2000. It had taken a year from start to finish.

MARBLE FLOOR INSTALLATION

In preparation for installing the marble floors, all that remained of the old subfloor assembly had to be removed and a new one built. The following season exterior plywood was added, and half-inch thick marble tiles were laid down with a waterproof adhesive. As with the parquet floors, the design patterns were chosen according to what was popular at the turn of the century.

CHAPTER 19

THE ARCH AND THE SWAN POND

The Boldt Castle Arch is patterned after the *Arc de Triomphe* in Paris. It was intended to be the entrance to the castle. It consisted of stone pillars that formed openings in four directions. The large opening between the river and the Swan Pond allowed boats to enter the protective mooring area for visitors' skiffs and motor craft.

Since the arch was built with cut stone, it required little restoration. Above it is a large stone roof topped by three impressive nine-foot tall, bronze life-sized stags that can be seen from a distance.

These stags were set in place with a crane mounted on a barge in 2001. It is believed that the original deer that once topped the arch had been sacrificed to the metal drive to support the war effort in 1942. The TIBA Board of Directors felt they ought to be replaced.

Rick Tague, of Bernier, Carr and Associates, created drawings from old photographs and drew up specifications for their replacements. The project was put out for bid and the challenge went to an artist in West Virginia who specialized in bronze works.

This gentleman created the full-sized stags on a pedestal in clay. It was an exciting day for Dale and Rick when they flew down to see them. The men approved them enthusiastically, and their creator shipped his clay molds to his foundry to be cast in bronze.

When they were finished, he brought them to the Yacht House in an enclosed truck. Ron Cyr, a local contractor with a crane and barge, carried them to Heart Island and set them in place.

The main docks were reserved for the tour boats carrying several hundred tourists. Commuter boats carrying two to four passengers were turned away. But these smaller craft were an important source of income and needed to be accommodated.

The shoreline of the Swan Pond was falling in. Workmen repaired it by driving steel into the riverbed to form a solid edge. Then it was backfilled with cement creating a landing area for the workboat and a Landing Craft Mechanized (LCM).

Developed early in World War II, the LCM could carry a battle tank or artillery pieces or heavy trucks and construction equipment to beaches that lacked port facilities. They were very versatile in wartime and proved so again during the Boldt Castle restoration.

Leon Rusho, Jr., of Clayton, owned an LCM which was used throughout the Thousand Islands. Masonry sand was immediately needed to begin repairing the stonework, and he was hired to provide it. Workmen loaded a dump truck and drove it aboard and then unloaded it at the island. Heavy debris was hauled back.

Once the shore line was fixed, a solid landing area was created to unload the workboat and the LCM. It also provided dockage for small boats.

Wooden antique boats at the Yacht House are no longer seaworthy but are nonetheless beautifully evocative of a bygone era. They were transported there aboard the LCM. After they entered the Yacht House, they were lifted by a sling and trolley system and put on display.

The LCM moved through the Arch at the Swan Pond to unload supplies with only inches to spare. Maneuvering such a large watercraft in that tight space was comparable to doing the breaststroke in a bathtub.

This landing craft was called upon regularly for heavy hauling during open water season.

The dock area at Swan Pond now welcomed all comers. The "welcome" was recognized by the local gull population as a roost. In due time they made such a mess, each day the crew used a gas-powered water pump on the barge to scrub the dock because wading through gull droppings would not be pleasant.

These unexpected odd jobs that occurred regularly exasperated Dale when he was trying to meet a timeline. But the visiting public must have an enjoyable experience, and his crew was determined to make that happen.

CHAPTER 20

THE CASTLE ROOF

The vantage point of the Saint Lawrence River, Boldt Castle rises like a magical kingdom lifted straight from George Boldt's memory of the castles he had seen in Germany. The castle roof covers a very large area. At 25,000 square feet, it's about half the size of a football field. With its many peaks, towers, chimneys, and spires, it resembles a small village.

Bats were present in the castle by the thousands. Every loose shingle or interior board that was moved disturbed them. One or one hundred bats flying around were distracting if not dangerous.

An exterminator, affectionately known as "Bat Man," was hired to evict them. Though he may have won several battles, the war was lost. Bats remain residents of Boldt Castle.

The castle roof was constructed of steel framing with two layers of clay tile. The top layer had to be replaced. The work could only be done in summer, and it was interrupted during the heaviest visitor season. Consequently, it took nearly four years to complete the task.

All things concerning work on the castle are measured

in tons, rather than pounds. The total weight of the roof is estimated to be about 790 tons.

The new tiles were transported from the Yacht House to Heart Island, using the LCM. A forklift loaded and unloaded the crates of tiles. When they reached the island, they were transported to the work area by a lawn tractor and utility trailer.

A ladder hoist carried these heavy loads to the roof. From that point on, the many tons of tile were moved by muscle power. To add to the burden, the old tiles had to be removed and brought down for proper disposal.

Working on these steep slopes always required foot support. A system of brackets was built to create a series of steps resembling terraces. When the work was completed, the brackets were removed as the workers descended.

The complexity of the roof design required drains to remove the rainwater. These drains would have to be kept clear of ice during the cold winter months. To accommodate this, a heat tape was installed in each one. Custom made tapes were fabricated on site. Electric power also had to be installed to each tape. It took about a month to complete this job.

The flat area above the dome was originally done in heavy glass blocks to allow natural light to the stained glass. Unfortunately, this system leaked, and it could not be sealed up. To correct the problem, a gabled greenhouse roof was constructed over the area. Other flat areas were covered with modern rubber materials.

CHAPTER 21

THE GOLDEN HELICOPTER

(as told by Dale Fikes)

A phone call interrupted my thoughts as I made plans for the day. "This is the Captain of the Forbes Yacht."

"Yeah, and I'm Robin Hood," I answered.

"I'm not kidding; I AM Captain of the Yacht."

"Okay, but I'm still not sure." I had been hoodwinked more than once, so I was taking no chances.

"I'll put the helicopter up right now and the pilot will circle the island."

"We see lots of helicopters around the island," I answered.

"How many gold ones do you see?" He paused and then added, "The pilot will rock from side to side as he comes around the west end of the island."

I waited at the Swan Pond. Sure enough, like a golden eagle, the beautiful helicopter appeared and tipped his wings as I waved my greeting.

Immediately, I received a call from the captain on the yacht.

"Do you believe me now?"

"I sure do," I replied, trying to save face.

Amidst his laughter, he said, "Mr. Forbes is not aboard today, but his staff would like to visit the castle."

Considering the questionable water depth for the safety of the yacht, we decided he should anchor and send the launch. The yacht crew arrived shortly thereafter aboard the Donzi runabout, obviously a very expensive boat. After disembarking, off they went to enjoy their first tour of Boldt Castle.

CHAPTER 22

ALSTER TOWER

(Known also as the Play House)

Construction of Alster Tower began in 1896. It opened for use in the summer of 1899. At first glance, the edifice seems to have been built on a pile of rocks. But looking closer, one sees what appears to be a rock pile is, in truth, a two-story foundation, constructed on rustic native stone. From that vantage point, a square tower rises sixty feet to where a parapet has been built on each corner. Handmade steps and walkways blend into the natural shape of the location, making the structure looks like it's part of the island itself. Inside the lowest level there's a bowling alley.

Dale's first visit to the tower was disconcerting. What a frightful mess! He'd never seen such a heap of rubble! The roof was gone. The inside overflowed with debris. Rubbish was strewn throughout the site. "Where do we begin to clean this up!" he grumbled to himself. He must figure out how to deal with this devastation and he had no time to waste. He'd try to come up with a plan that very evening.

Early the next morning he returned to the tower with his crew. They immediately set to work gutting the tower and its environs of the fallout of decades of neglect and decay. Working together, they separated the debris into piles for the landfill or recycling. They would have to be transported to the mainland later.

Now that the site was cleaned up, to prevent further deterioration, they must replace the crumbling mortar between the stone. This procedure is called repointing.

Originally the flat square roof atop the sixty-foot tower was covered with asphalt. The roof leaked and the frame had rotted and fallen mostly inside the tower. They'd have to build a new one.

Safety was a prime concern for Dale, and elevated work always presented additional danger. His crew knew that. They did not have to be reminded to stand clear as others hoisted heavy timbers up for the new roof, using a rope and pulley system.

Once the new roof was framed and a deck installed, the men covered it with new rubber material that should last for many years. What appears today to be a paved patio is really the roof of the bowling alley in the basement.

The years flew by. Sometime in the 1990s, Dale discovered the walls were cracking. Puzzled, he pondered the possible causes. The work done by his crew was always of the highest quality and was not suspect. There had not been an earthquake. Other natural causes were ruled out. There was only one logical explanation. Alster Tower was settling. It had been constructed on solid rocks. How could that happen?

Dale scratched his head pondering the situation. He could think of only one possibility. Heart Island must be splitting apart! He hoped his conclusion was wrong, but he couldn't find anything else that might cause those cracks.

One lifetime was not long enough to solve all the problems associated with Boldt Castle and Heart Island. Dale's retirement came before this mystery could be addressed. The time had come to get a full night's sleep.

After his retirement in 2002, the management hired a diver to investigate the areas along the shoreline of the tower. Erosion seemed to be a possibility. After making his inspection, the diver grinned as he pulled off his mask. "You'll be surprised to know what I've discovered! The edge of that mighty tower was built over open water. It's supported on wooden cribs!"

Heart Island was not splitting in two. Nevertheless, a way to stabilize the tower had to be devised. A contractor with a barge-mounted pile driver created a form by driving large flat pieces of metal, called sheets, into the riverbed to enclose the crib area beneath the tower foundation. Then, liquid cement was poured into the form to encapsulate the area. The hardened cement created a solid masonry foundation and became an integral part of the island.

This difficult, but essential, work stabilized the tower structure and stopped the walls from cracking. Now the crew could get back to renovating the tower.

At this writing (2020), Alster Tower is undergoing TIBA's largest restoration project on Heart Island.

CHAPTER 23

THE LIGHT

On one side of Alster Tower stood an ornate, iron tripod structure. Towering six or seven feet skyward, its extended iron arms each ended in a large hook with wire protruding from the top. Could this have been a lamp post? Hmm? Dale wondered what it looked like.

One day a stranger phoned him. "Are you familiar with the pedestal near Alster Tower?" he asked.

"I noticed it, but I don't know what it supported," Dale told him.

"I know," said the stranger. "It was a light pedestal. It had four arms, each holding a hanging light. As a young man I saw visitors steal anything they could remove from the castle.

"One day when I was back at the castle, I noticed all but one of the lights had disappeared." He caught his breath and continued. "I took the last one home, hoping to return it if the castle was ever restored." He paused. "If you'll keep my name out of this, I'll give it to you."

"OKAY! That's a promise!"

The caller continued. “Go to the coffee shop in Clayton tomorrow morning at eight o’clock. Park your station wagon and leave it unlocked. Go inside and enjoy a cup of coffee. Don’t come out for twenty minutes.”

In the restoration business, this was like finding a treasure chest or a pot of gold. Dale trusted this wasn’t a plan to steal his vehicle. Following the stranger’s instructions, he showed up right on time the next morning.

Like a kid waiting for Santa, he impatiently watched the minutes tick by. At 8:19, he gulped his last mouthful of coffee, walked out to his parked vehicle with giant strides, and anxiously opened the back door. Inside he found a heart-shaped wrought iron basket enclosing a glass globe. On the top was a ring designed to hang onto the hooked arm of the pedestal. A tin roof protected the assembly from the weather.

As he headed off to work, Dale envisioned how four of these pieces attached to the pedestal would make a unique chandelier. He couldn’t wait to show his crew what he had brought home.

Following the suggestion by one of his men, Dale contacted John Scarlett of Rossie, a respected area blacksmith. They made an appointment to meet a few days later. When they met, John extended a calloused palm that was indicative of hours swinging a hammer.

Knowing his reputation for good work, Dale wasted no time in small talk. “Can you reproduce this piece?” he asked while handing it to him.

John turned the strange thing over in his hands and paused. "What is this thing?"

Dale explained, "When assembled, four of these will replace the lamp at Alster Tower."

The quality of the work and the challenge of doing what Dale wanted him to do excited John. Speaking with enthusiasm, he said, "First, I'll have to take it apart to make jigs and tools. I'll use the old pieces for patterns."

With a handshake and thank you, the deal was made. Within a few weeks, John had finished his work and called Dale to come get it. He showed up the next day and took his treasure home.

After installing new wires, the original light, dating back to 1900, was once again illuminating the night on Heart Island.

CHAPTER 24

THE POWER HOUSE

George Boldt knew he would need power, and plenty of it, to keep the castle lights burning and to entertain the many guests he and his gracious wife Louise would host. He designed the Power House to supply adequate power on special occasions as well as to meet day-to-day living requirements.

The Power House at the east end of Heart Island was built to produce electric power to the island and to pump water up to the castle. Rebuilding it was a monumental undertaking. In 1938, flames sparked by a fireworks display destroyed the tower roofs and wooden interior. With no protective cover overhead, rain and snow combined with heavy frosts weakened the stone and the walls tumbled into the St. Lawrence River.

Because of the devastation inside, trees with a diameter of six inches had sprouted and grown tall on the floor of the second story. The interior was filled with rubble made from mortar, glass, and several hundred pounds of burned and rusted nails.

The picturesque two-story, arched stone bridge had totally collapsed into the water. The workers designed a supporting base form for it, which was really an arched stairway with a steep angle to the second story. Structural steel arched beams with decking supported the heavy stonework.

The Power House was surrounded by stones that had fallen into the water. A piece of heavy equipment was acquired to retrieve the stones. A barge-mounted crane with a clamshell was brought to the site to pick up the stones as directed by a diver in the water. Radio contact by the diver and crane operator enabled them to work together and retrieve all the stone within a few days.

To preserve the authenticity of the stone towers and the arched bridge, the contractors referred to original photographs of them when they were in place.

Another bridge was constructed with a level walkway to allow easy access to all visitors.

A tunnel housed water pipes and power cables leading to the castle. It also contained drainage tiles.

One morning two men from the Franklin Motor Car Company Museum in Syracuse, New York, contacted Dale. "We have some old electrical generating equipment similar to what would have been used in the original Power House," they said. "We no longer have space to store it. We'd be happy to donate it to you. The only cost for you would be $800 for shipping."

Dale accepted their gracious offer without hesitation.

Conical roofs and dormers like those originally on the Power House were a carpenter's nightmare. But it was important to build the new ones according to the original designs. The clock tower had three clock faces that could be seen from any side. Keeping with the original design, all their roofs were covered in red cedar shingles. With the bright sun shining on them, they could be seen for miles. Thus, the Power House, or Water Castle, as it was sometimes called, became a major attraction on Heart Island. With its five conical towers, the Power House presents a fairyland vision, reminiscent of Disneyland.

SNAKES

Water snakes are native to the Thousand Islands region, and Heart Island is one of their habitats. Since they are shy, nonvenomous, and seldom visible, they pose no concern. However, on one occasion, some snakes made their way into an electrical box and interrupted power to the castle. When the box was opened to find the cause of the power outage, the worker recoiled. "Fried snakes!" he yelled.

Several snakes had found their way into the box. The lights flickered each time one met its doom. The short circuit increased, and the interruption became more frequent. The problem was solved by making the circuit box snakeproof.

CHAPTER 25

THE 4TH OF JULY

No community takes our nation's birthday more seriously than Alexandria Bay. Its fireworks display is recognized as the largest and finest in the area. Because it's fired from Heart Island, it attracts boaters from Canada as well as the United States, making it truly an international celebration enjoyed by the two nations. Boats quite literally cover the water like stepping stones.

But danger lurks where there are fireworks. The disastrous fire that destroyed the Power House in 1938 during the fireworks has not been forgotten. Consequently, every 4th of July thereafter a crew was dispatched to the castle to disperse would-be trespassers and to post a fire watch on Heart Island.

A fire watch was posted atop Alster Tower as well as on the fourth-floor balcony of the castle. The firemen carried hand-operated pumps.

A barge-mounted fire pump was kept at the dock to protect dockside buildings since they were covered with cedar shingles. The shingles were the tinder that could catch a spark with disastrous results. The Alex Bay Fireboat stayed by the vulnerable Power House and kept it wet during the entire event.

At the conclusion of the gigantic fireworks display all was safe and the blasts of a hundred horns demonstrated the crowd's approval.

CHAPTER 26

THE HENNERY

George Boldt was proud of his prize fowl, which were housed in a stone tower-like structure called a hennery. The top section served as a dovecote for his homing pigeons.

In 1977 all that remained of the building was a crumbled stone structure with stones enough lying on the ground to rebuild it. Visitors picked their way carefully through the fallen stone and debris to get inside in search of anything they could take away of historic value.

A huge vat inside the hennery was added to collect rainwater for Boldt's proposed greenhouse nearby.

Because of time constraints, during the first stages of reconstruction the hennery area was closed off to the public. It was completed during the 1992-1993 season.

The reconstructed hennery looks like an over-sized silo with what appears to be a giant wooden birdhouse atop it. This octagonal dovecote is eight feet tall with multiple openings for the doves to enter their nesting boxes.

Access to the nests was gained by a hinged door on the back of each nest. An inside ladder from the ground level reached to the floor of the dovecote. Nestlings could be removed for eating. With its pointed peak and broad overhang at the edges, the roof resembles a giant witch's hat.

CHAPTER 27

DALE'S SWAN SONG THE CASTLE DOME

Dale Fikes is a dreamer, and he dreams big. Accepting responsibility for restoring Heart Island properties required a vision of major proportions. Early on, he had envisioned a beautiful lofty dome above the Grand Staircase. He looked forward to working on such a project.

But other areas were a higher priority. Thousands of guests were already visiting Heart Island each year and the numbers continued to grow. Each season the grounds must be made attractive and the buildings safe for the hordes who were boated across the St. Lawrence River to the castle grounds.

Year by year the work progressed steadily, creating colorful garden paths as well as carrying out interior restoration. The public noticed, spread the word, and thousands more came to visit the next year.

Twenty-three years after Dale became Clerk of the Works, the castle dome was given top priority. At last he could bring to life his dream. Bernier, Carr and Associates were hired to present a design for it. That company assigned recognized architect, Rick Tague, and stained-glass expert, Julia Sloan, to design the basic structure and the glass artwork. Since neither details nor drawings of Boldt's original intentions for the dome were ever found, Rick and Julia were free to create a design according to what they felt would be most appropriate for the world-famous landmark.

While Rick and Julie were working on the design, Dale scouted out companies that might be able to do the work. He concluded that Brennan Stained Glass of Syracuse had the capabilities to create what he had in mind. He contacted the company and set up a date to meet a representative over lunch.

After meeting, greeting, and eating, Dale presented his idea to the rep. His guest could not hide his enthusiasm for the project, and he was eager to share it with his company. As the two set a date to meet again, the Brennan rep said, "Let me pick up the tab."

"No way," said Dale. "It's my pleasure." He had a hunch that TIBA would be receiving a bid for the job. If the bid was accepted, the contractor would be asked to sign a Non-Collusion Affidavit. He could do that with a clear conscience.

As Dale hoped would happen, Brennan submitted a bid to TIBA for the work and the company was given the contract. By then, Rick and Julie had finished their design and created patterns for it.

The contract was signed, and the patterns were given to Brennan Stained Glass. Once they were received, Scott Brennan set to work tweaking them because of the curvature, since glass does not bend.

This task was not child's play, nor are the structures in a dome random pieces of glass fitted together. Each piece must be designed to fit into its own position, just as the pieces of a quilt are carefully cut and sewed into their proper places. To form the art pattern for each piece according to the shape of the dome when you're working with rigid, unforgiving glass is a demanding job!

The castle dome consisted of 16 framed sections in the original steel "arches," fitted together somewhat like the ribs on an umbrella. These arches were the only clue to the intentions of the architect who designed the castle. Viewed in a cross-section, they resembled an upside-down T-shaped form, designed to support the glass on either side.

An elevated platform was built beneath the dome for the installers. At times they lay on their backs to do their work.

To assemble stained glass to the desired shape, it was necessary to work with a mold. The molds for these segments were constructed of 1/8-inch plywood strips that would bend easily. These strips, held by clamps and braces, were laminated to form a solid panel. Each 16-foot panel was divided into three slender pie-shaped sections. The result was forty-eight sections that had to fit together perfectly.

With these molds in place, the workers inside the dome marked each line for the new glass. When viewed from below all lines must appear continuous across the frames.

Each segment was then fitted with a plywood form to protect its shape and prevent damage. These 48 sections were mounted on plywood forms which served as shipping crates. They were carried down the stairs and transported to Brennan's Syracuse studio to have the glass assembled.

At the studio the next step was to draw the patterns on paper for each individual piece of glass. Then the glass was cut to fit each one precisely and was assembled in an identical pattern in the wood mold.

The glass was held together with a lead strip called "caming." Every joint around each piece, large or small, is soldered to make a glass sheet. Stained glass assemblies are not rigid, so it was necessary to add reinforcing bars to strengthen them. Once that was done all the panels were sealed and cleaned, crated, and returned to the Castle.

Their journey from Syracuse to Boldt Castle was made by trucks, barge, and tractor, with the final 700 steps up four stories completed by sheer muscle power. And once they reached the dome area, their only access to the inside was through a small window.

The work of installing the 48 panels into the dome had to be done mostly at night when there were no visitors present. "Safety first" was the workers' rule. If a screwdriver accidentally dropped onto somebody from ninety feet, he could be killed instantly. So, no one was allowed in that area when the work was in progress. Once all the panels were aligned, clipped and soldered in place, the work platform was removed.

The size of the dome cannot be fully appreciated from a distance. A good comparison is to imagine a Tiffany lamp shade the size of a living room, twenty feet in diameter and seven feet tall.

From the day it was installed that beautiful dome drew Dale's attention like a magnet. Every time he entered the castle thereafter, his gaze automatically rose upward to it. His gentle sigh and some occasional tears of deep appreciation assured him his dream had come true.

The castle dome was truly Dale's "Swan Song."

CHAPTER 28

SAYING "GOODBYE"

At Dale's last meeting, a week before his retirement, the Thousand Islands Bridge Authority Board of Directors presented him with a plaque thanking him for his years of dedication and service. That plaque is on display in the Billiard's Room in the Boldt Castle.

Resolution of Appreciation to

Dale F. Fikes

for his Dedication and Stewardship of the

Boldt Facilities Rehabilitation Program

as

Director, Engineering, Construction & Maintenance

1977-2002

WHEREAS, with the Authority's 1976 acquisition of the historic Boldt Castle, Heart Island and Boldt Yacht House properties, hereinafter referred to as the Boldt Facilities, to foster continued public visitation and enjoyment of such facilities, a major repair and rehabilitation program was required, and

WHEREAS, to oversee the Boldt Facilities rehabilitation efforts, Dale F. Fikes was employed by the Authority in 1977 as Director, Engineering, Construction and Maintenance, and served with exceptional competence in such capacity until his retirement in 2002 and

WHEREAS, as the result of his twenty-five years of dedicated stewardship of the rehabilitation program, the Boldt Facilities have been transformed into a premier attraction for the enjoyment of current and future generations.

NOW THEREFORE BE IT RESOLVED, that the Authority, as its proper act and deed, records on its permanent records, its sincere appreciation to Dale F. Fikes for his outstanding dedication and service as Director, Engineering, Construction and Maintenance, and

FURTHER, BE IT RESOLVED, that this resolution shall be prepared in an appropriate form for presentation to Dale F. Fikes and for the purpose of permanent display at the Boldt Facilities.

By unanimous vote of the

Thousand Islands Bridge

Authority May 16, 2002

ADDENDUM
PEOPLE WHO WORKED WITH DALE

Dale appreciated the many talented people he worked with through 25 years of restoring Bold Castle. He was concerned that he might not remember everybody. Yet, he felt it would be unfair not to give credit to the ones he did remember because they worked with him as a team. If he inadvertently omitted someone, he regrets it.

Foremost on his list are Russel Wilcox and the Board of Directors of the Thousand Islands Bridge Authority. Following fast on their heels are the Bridge employees with whom he worked.

CONTRACTORS AND SPECIALIZED WORKERS

Bernier, Carr & Assoc.	Architect – Rick Tague
Brad Cosman	Mike Putnam
Brennan Stained Glass	Scott Brennan
CEF Construction	Gordon Fayhe
Curtis Furniture	Peter Curtis
Dunaway T. Morgan	Dave Dunaway
Earl Rumsey Durand	Sculptor

Grenadier Construction	Dave Detwiller
GYMO	Architect – Steve Yaussi
John Scarlett	Blacksmith
Junior Rusho	LCM Owner
Law Brothers	Blair Law
Pearson Timmerman	Dennis Jaero
Purcell Construction	Mark Purcell
Raulli Ornamental Ironworks	Richard Alexander
	Ron Cyr
Umstead Construction	Brian Umstead

DALE'S OTHER CO-WORKERS

Brian Hanson	Bridge Employee
Brian Salisbury	Director, Boldt Facilities Operations, Maintenance and Construction
Dale Leeson and Manny Slate	Castle and Power House windows, docks and everything else
G. Brian Umstead	Grand Stairway woodwork
Jim Bacon	Golf Club Manager
John Umstead	Bridge Employee
Ken Hunter	Carpentry, masonry work & windows

Kevin Gillette	Operated potable and water systems
Michael Gibbs	Marble stairs, treads, risers & flooring
Richard Dack	Construction and Maintenance
Ron Timmerman	Bridge Employee
Shane Sanford	Former Castle Manager
WWII Veteran Grounds Keepers	Andy Rae, George Carrol & Ivan Strough

BOLDT CASTLE TRIVIA

1. At the height of construction, along with his stone quarry and farms, it is estimated George Boldt employed three hundred people. Seventy-five of them were stone cutters. The craftsmen worked ten hours per day, six days a week, and were paid $1.50 per day. Such high wages were unheard of at the turn of the century and it upset the local business community.

2. Boldt Castle has approximately 100 rooms, 30 bathrooms and fireplaces.

3. There are 709 windows in the historical structures. That's 348 in the castle; 213 in the Yacht House; 97 in Alster Tower; 43 in the Power House, and 8 in the Dove Cote.

IN RETROSPECT

Boldt Castle's restoration will never be finished. The tremendous popularity of this nearly 120-year-old landmark in the Thousand Islands draws as many as 200,000 visitors each season. The tramp of all their feet brings wear and tear to what has been restored in the previous years. The costs of upkeep are high and that limits how fast the Thousand Islands Bridge Authority can move forward toward bringing to fruition George Boldt's dream plans for his island castle.

Nevertheless, those who return each year will be pleased with the changes they see.

May God bless Dale Fikes for his twenty-five years of dedicated work.

He came! He saw! He conquered!